In My Backyard

I SEE A FROG

By Alex Appleby

Gareth Stevens Publishing

Please visit our website, www.garethstevens.com. For a free color catalog of all our high-quality books, call toll free 1-800-542-2595 or fax 1-877-542-2596.

Library of Congress Cataloging-in-Publication Data

Appleby, Alex.
 I see a frog / Alex Appleby.
     p. cm. — (In my backyard)
 Includes index.
 ISBN 978-1-4339-8552-2 (pbk.)
 ISBN 978-1-4339-8553-9 (6-pack)
 ISBN 978-1-4339-8551-5 (library binding)
 1. Frogs—Juvenile literature. I. Title.
 QL668.E2A66 2013
 597.8'9—dc23

                                    2012020692

First Edition

Published in 2013 by
Gareth Stevens Publishing
111 East 14th Street, Suite 349
New York, NY 10003

Editor: Ryan Nagelhout
Designer: Katelyn Londino

Photo credits: Cover, p. 1 Andre Goncalves/Shutterstock.com; p. 5 Oxford Scientific/Oxford Scientific/Getty Images; p. 7 Amee Cross/Shutterstock.com; pp. 9, 21, 23, 24 (spots) iStockphoto/Thinkstock.com; p. 11 Andrew F. Kazmierski/Shutterstock.com; pp. 13, 24 (webbed) Donald Mallalieu/Shutterstock.com; pp. 15, 24 (tadpole) koko-tewan/Shutterstock.com; p. 17 © iStockphoto.com/AttaBoyLuther; p. 19 Dr. Morley Read/Shutterstock.com.

Printed in the United States of America

CPSIA compliance information: Batch #CW13GS: For further information contact Gareth Stevens, New York, New York at 1-800-542-2595.

Contents

A frog likes to hop!

It has long legs.
These help it jump
very far.

7

A frog loves water!

9

It likes to live
near ponds.

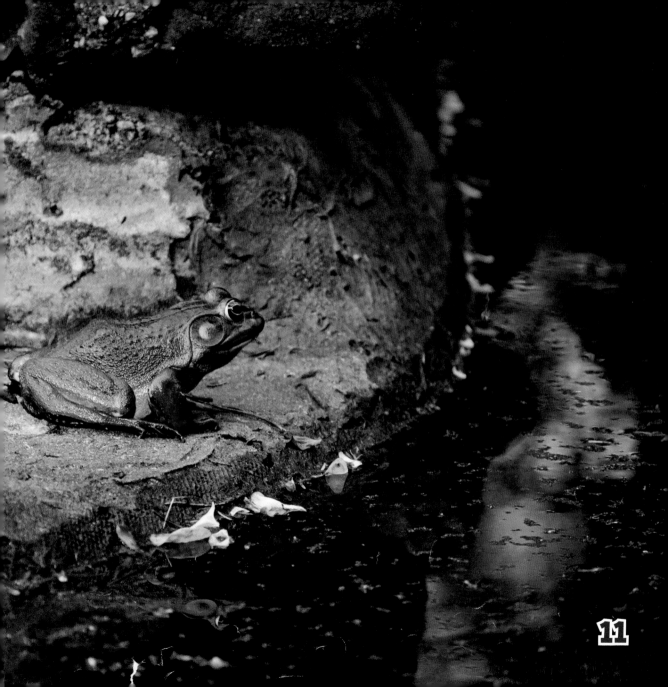

11

Its feet are webbed.
This helps it swim.

13

Baby frogs start life in water. These are called tadpoles.

A tadpole has a tail
to help it swim.

17

Soon it grows legs.
Its tail falls off before
it becomes an adult.

19

A northern leopard frog
has big black spots.
It likes to hop
in the grass.

21

Bullfrogs are very loud!
They have deep voices.

23

Words to Know

spots   tadpole   webbed

Index

24